Cartwheels:

A Workbook For Children

Who Have Been

Sexually Abused

ii

CARTWHEELS: A WORKBOOK FOR CHILDREN WHO HAVE BEEN SEXUALLY ABUSED

Phyllis Spinal-Robinson, L.C.S.W.

and

Randi Easton Wickham, L.S.W.

Jalice Publishers
Notre Dame, Indiana

CARTWHEELS:

A WORKBOOK FOR CHILDREN WHO HAVE BEEN SEXUALLY ABUSED.

Published by Jalice Publishers, P.O. Box 455, Notre Dame, IN 46556

Library of Congress Cataloging-in-Publication Data
Spinal-Robinson, Phyllis and Wickham, Randi Easton.

Cartwheels: A Workbook for Children Who Have Been Sexually Abused.

1. Sexually abused children. 2. Incest victims. 3. Mental health — children.
I. Spinal-Robinson, Phyllis. II. Wickham, Randi Easton. III. Title.

1992
ISBN 0-9627375-1-8

Dedication and Acknowledgements

We would like to dedicate *Cartwheels* to all kids who have been hurt by sexual abuse and who are so very brave and courageous.

We are grateful for the the therapists who have believed the children and who are helping them with their healing journey.

We would like to thank the following:

Our husbands,...Stephen, for his enthusiasm, humor, encouragement, and emotional support...Byron, for loving encouragement and technical computer assistance...Randi's sister, Kelly, for her encouragement, affection, and creativity...Randi's nephew and niece, Gabrielle and Eric Easton, for beautiful artwork which is included in this workbook...Gabrielle, for the cover of this workbook...Michael Hayes, our artist friend, who provided invaluable expertise and assistance...Des Plaines Valley Community Center, where we've received much of our training and the clinical experience that enabled us to create this workbook.... Our publishers and editor for the dedicated commitment in the field of sexual abuse and to this project...and most importantly, our clients who have taught us what bravery truly is.

Introduction For Kids

Dear Kids,

This workbook has been written especially for you. It will help you and your therapist to talk about the sexual abuse that you experienced, and it will help you to understand your feelings. We have talked to many kids who have been sexually abused, and we have found that these exercises can be very helpful. We hope that you also enjoy the games and exercises. They can be very exciting and a lot of fun. If an exercise is too hard, do the best you can and feel proud of what you've done.

We hope you learn that you can ask for help and feel better. Getting to know yourself and learning how to be your own best friend is a very important part of growing up!

Sincerely,

Randi & Phyllis

Gabrielle East

Table Of Contents

Checklist

Most kids who have been sexually abused will experience many emotional and physical reactions to the abuse. This is very normal. You are not alone in how you feel. It will probably take a while for you to feel okay and safe again. This checklist will help you and your therapist to notice the kind of reaction you might be having. See how many of these items seem to fit for you and place an X in the blank of those that do.

Sometimes kids who are sexually abused...

1.___ Have stomachaches

2.___ Have bad dreams or nightmares

3.___ Imagine that all their friends know what happened

4.___ Imagine that no one will like them

5.___ Feel like it's their fault

6.___ Feel confused because they may like and trust the person who abused them

7.___ Have trouble sleeping

8.___ Are afraid to tell anyone what happened to them

9.___ Are afraid they'll get punished or get in trouble if they tell what happened

10.___ Have been told something bad will happen to them if they tell

11.___ Believe that their body is ugly or dirty

12.___ Have problems eating

13.___ Have difficulty paying attention

14.___ Have problems in school

Measuring Scale:

This measuring scale will help you to know yourself. It will be repeated several times so that you and your therapist can be aware of how you're thinking, feeling, and behaving.

<u>Circle One</u>

I feel scared.	Always	Often	Sometimes	Never
I like myself.	Always	Often	Sometimes	Never
I feel sad.	Always	Often	Sometimes	Never
I'm afraid.	Always	Often	Sometimes	Never
I'm embarrassed.	Always	Often	Sometimes	Never
I feel angry.	Always	Often	Sometimes	Never
I'm happy.	Always	Often	Sometimes	Never
I get upset.	Always	Often	Sometimes	Never
I have nightmares.	Always	Often	Sometimes	Never
I'm a good person.	Always	Often	Sometimes	Never
I get mad.	Always	Often	Sometimes	Never
I'm shy.	Always	Often	Sometimes	Never
I have friends.	Always	Often	Sometimes	Never
I like other kids.	Always	Often	Sometimes	Never
People like me.	Always	Often	Sometimes	Never
My family likes me.	Always	Often	Sometimes	Never
I would be a good friend to have.	Always	Often	Sometimes	Never
I'm excited about growing up.	Always	Often	Sometimes	Never

Secrets

A secret is something that someone tells you and asks you not to tell anyone else about. There are different kinds of secrets. Some are okay and some are not okay. Usually, secrets that are not okay leave you feeling uncomfortable or confused.

What do you think about the following secrets?

Are they okay or not okay?

Circle okay or not okay

1. A friend tells you about a surprise birthday party being planned for someone. You are asked not to tell about the surprise.

okay   not okay

2. A friend stole something from the store and asks you not to tell anyone.

okay   not okay

3. Someone you know and trust touches your private parts and asks you not to tell anyone.

okay   not okay

4. Another kid cheats on a test at school and asks you not to tell.

okay   not okay

5. Your brother buys a present for your mom and asks you not to tell.

okay   not okay

6. Someone you know and trust touches your private parts or asks you to touch their private parts. You are told that something bad will happen if you tell anyone about it.

okay   not okay

Can you think of some other secrets? Write them down.

Are these secrets okay or not okay?

_____

_____

_____

_____

FEELING RESPONSIBLE FOR THE ABUSE

Kids should never be sexually abused! There are many different kinds of sexual abuse. Sometimes the abuse involves touching, but there are other ways in which kids may be abused. If you are confused by a touch or by something else that happens to you, talk with your therapist, parent, or someone you trust. Adults should never touch kids in sexual ways. It is wrong, but sadly, many kids are sexually abused. Kids shouldn't be taken advantage of. Sometimes kids are hurt because they believe they should trust adults, especially adults to whom they are close. An adult should never take advantage of a kid's trust in him or her.

N E V E R !

Sometimes kids feel responsible or to blame for having been sexually abused. They may feel that they should have been able to fight back or stop the abuse in some way. They often mistakenly believe that it was something about them or something they did that caused the abuse. Many times kids are confused or afraid, so they do not tell anyone about the abuse. For all of these reasons, kids will often feel that they are to blame. This is not true! Kids are never responsible or to blame for the abuse.

N E V E R !

Are there some ways that you feel responsible or to blame for the abuse?
List any:

_____

_____

_____

_____

_____

_____

Who are some people you could talk to about these feelings? List some
people whom you trust.

_____

_____

_____

_____

_____

Other Kids' Stories

1. David, age 8, was often taken care of by John, a friend of his father. David felt that John was a special friend. John often brought David presents, played games with him, and paid attention to his feelings and needs. David had always wished for an older man he could look up to because his father was often busy and didn't spend much time with him. David felt very close to John and spent a lot of time with him.

One day John took David to a park and showed him pictures of people having sex. David was very confused and didn't know what to do. John told him he had better not tell because he would get in big trouble. John also gave him a nice present that day, a video game that he had always wanted. David was afraid to tell his parents. He felt ashamed and was afraid that he would get in a lot of trouble if he told anyone what had happened to him. Also, he accepted the gift and believed this meant he couldn't tell.

2. Amy, age 10, was very close to her father. They would often talk and spend time alone together. Her father told her that they had a very "special" relationship. He would often tell her that he was lonely and that she was the one who helped him not to feel lonely. One night while Amy's mother was at work, Amy's father sexually abused her. Amy was confused and afraid. Amy's father tried to tell her that this was o.k. and that all fathers taught their daughters this way. He also told her that it was her fault because she hadn't told him to stop. He told Amy that if she told anyone, the whole family would be broken apart. He tried to make Amy feel that she must have wanted it to happen. Amy believed she couldn't tell because of all the trouble it would cause. She was also afraid it would get her father in trouble.

3. Cindy, age 6, liked to play with several kids in the neighborhood. One of her friends, Peter, had an older sister named Sally, age 14. One day while Cindy was at Peter's house, Sally asked her to come into her room so she could show her something. Sally touched Cindy's private parts. Afterwards, Sally told Cindy that she had better not tell anyone because no one would believe her. She also threatened her and told her she would harm her and her family if she told anyone about what had happened. Sally told her that Cindy had wanted it to happen because she had come into her room. Cindy was very upset and scared. She didn't know what to do.

What do you think about the stories on page 6? Do you feel the kid was ever to blame for what happened? Why or why not? Do you recognize anything similar or different about these kids' situations and your own? If so, what…

_____

_____

_____

_____

Please talk to your therapist or an adult you trust if you have any feelings that you are to blame for your abuse. These feelings can be hurtful and can get in the way of feeling better. Sometimes it takes a while for these feelings to go away.

You deserve the time to heal.

SOME FACTS:

Both boys and girls are sexually abused. Sometimes boys have a harder time than girls telling anyone about the abuse.

People who sexually abuse children can be either male or female. When kids are abused by their mom, dad, or another relative, it can be very confusing, especially if some of the sexual touching felt good.

Kids often feel especially confused if the person abusing them is a parent, relative, close friend, or trusted person who doesn't threaten them but asks them to keep this their "special secret."

Sometimes we love people, but we don't like the things they do to us.

You can still love a person even if you don't like the things they do to you.

Positive Messages

Here is a list of messages that might help you to feel better.

<u>Try saying these messages out loud!</u>

1. I am absolutely not to blame.

2. What happened was not my fault.

3. Adults should never touch kids in a sexual way.

4. I have a right to my own body and to decide who touches it.

5. There is nothing I did that caused the abuse.

6. I am not alone. Other kids have had the same experience.

7. People care about me.

8. I care about myself.

9. As I talk about how I was sexually abused, I will feel better.

10. The only person to blame for my abuse was the abuser.

11. I have a right to my feelings about the abuse.

12. I deserve to feel better, and I am going to take good care of myself!!!!!!
What other messages could you add?

_____

_____

_____

_____

_____

Pick a message for the day. Pick the one that you would most like to hear.

Your Body

Sometimes kids who have been abused have special worries and questions about their bodies. It can be very helpful to talk with a parent, teacher, counselor, school nurse, or family doctor about these feelings.

Kids sometimes worry that their bodies may be hurt, damaged, or different because of the abuse. Kids sometimes also worry that other people will be able to tell that they've been abused just by looking at them. This isn't true, but it is good to talk to an adult about any fears you might have.

Your body is good, and it belongs to you. There are some exercises in this book that will help you get to know and understand your body. It is important to make friends with your body and take good care of it.

What questions or worries do you have about your body?

_____

_____

_____

_____

_____

_____

Please talk to someone you feel comfortable with about
these questions or worries.

Your Body

Can you fill in and name the body parts using this picture?

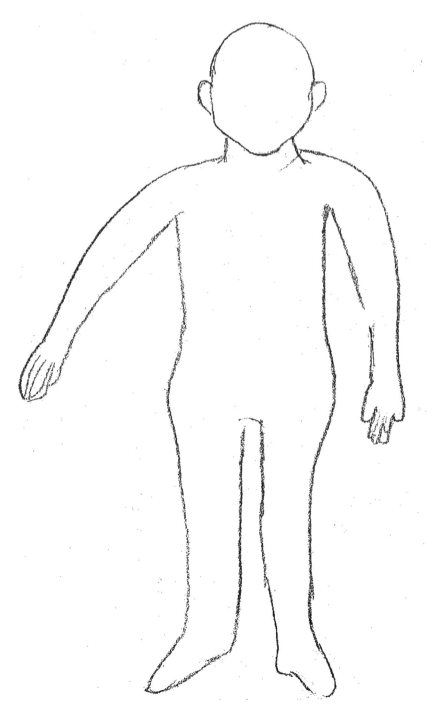

Your body is good. Your body belongs to you. Your body will be healthy
and feel good if you treat it

with lots of TLC

(tender loving care)

Your Body

Ways to feel good about your body:

1. Do some stretching exercises.

2. Lie down and breathe deeply. Feel your breath and imagine it calming your whole body.

3. Put on some music. Move to the music.

4. Get some exercise: swim, run, go for a nature walk.

5. Join a movement class: dance, martial arts, gymnastics, etc.

6. Get involved in a sport.

Can you think of other ways that you can take care
of and feel good about your body?

_____

_____

_____

_____

_____

Feelings in Your Body

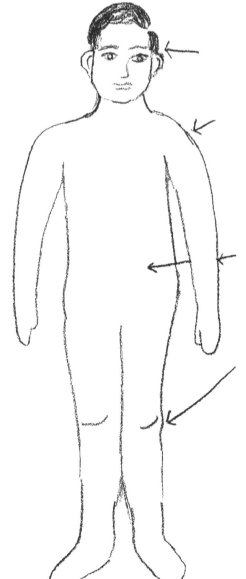

"My head is spinning."

"I've got a chip on my shoulder."

"I've got butterflies in my stomach."

"My knees are wobbly."

People often have feelings in their bodies. Can you show where you have feelings in your body? You can use different colors for different feelings and color them in.

anger   embarrassment   sadness   fear   surprise

nervousness   confusion   excitement

Kids' Pictures

Today [ICE] Free Ice cream

Dog

I Love To Dance

Use Your Imagination: A Relaxation Exercise

Here is a relaxation exercise you can practice with your therapist. Once you have learned this exercise, you may wish to do it with a parent or friend or alone.

To begin: get in a very comfortable position,
relax, take some deep breaths, and close your eyes.

Imagine you are somewhere very beautiful and quiet. It may be somewhere you've really been or it may be a place in your dreams. Is it a green forest, a park, or a mountain top with a running stream or waterfall? It might be near the ocean or a desert with cactus flowers. Maybe it's in the woods somewhere with the smell of pine trees. You pick the place.

Are you alone or is there a close friend or family member there with you? Keep taking deep breaths and relax your entire body. This is a place where you feel relaxed, calm, and safe. It is your place....a place where there are no worries. What are you doing in this place? Are you resting, sitting, strolling, or briskly walking? What do you see, smell, and hear? It is your place....your safe place.

**Now that you've found this place, remember you
can always carry it with you.**

It is a place for you to relax and feel better!

You can go there whenever you want.

Anger

Kids often react to being sexually abused by becoming angry.

Anger is a normal reaction to being abused. You have a right to be angry about what happened to you. While it is okay to be angry, it is not okay to express your anger by hurting yourself or someone else. It is very important to find safe ways to show your anger.

Safe ways to be angry:

1. **Do an anger dance. Pretend the floor is the abuser's face.**

2. **Punch pillows.**

3. **Hit a punching bag.**

4. **Write a letter telling how angry you are. (You may or may not decide to mail it.)**

5. **Get some exercise: go for a run or hit a ball against a wall.**

6. **Do a silent scream.**

7. **Talk with your therapist or someone you trust about your anger.**

8. **Make bombs out of clay or paper and throw them at a target.**

What are some other ways that you can safely show your anger?

_____

_____

_____

_____

_____

Ways to Cope:
Things to do when I'm feeling afraid or overwhelmed:

1. Take several deep breaths.

2. Find a family member or a special friend to talk to.

3. Say a prayer.

4. Close my eyes. Use my imagination to go to my safe place.

5. Say some positive messages.

6. Listen to some music that I like.

7. Take a walk, play a game, or do some exercise that will help my body to feel more relaxed.

List other ways to cope:

_____

_____

_____

_____

_____

Draw a picture showing how you were sexually abused or showing how you felt about being sexually abused.

Letter to the Abuser

To:_____   Date:_____

From:_____

There are a lot of things I want to say to you! I used to feel _____
_____. After you began to abuse
me, I felt_____

_____

_____

I thought _____

_____

_____

When I think of what you did to me, I feel _____

_____

_____

If you ever try to abuse me again, I will_____

_____

_____

I am safe now because _____

_____

_____

Signed: _____

Write another letter to the person who abused you. Say whatever you feel like saying:

To: _____   Date: _____

From: _____

_____

_____

_____

_____

_____

_____

_____

_____

_____

_____

_____

_____

_____

_____

_____

Signed:_____

Other Kids' Letters

Dear Mike,

I hate you for what you did to me. I hope you go to jail.

I miss you. I'm really mad at you. Thank you for the presents you gave me. I hope you're not mad at me.

Billy

◆ ◆ ◆ ◆ ◆ ◆ ◆ ◆ ◆ ◆

Sometimes kids have both good and bad feelings about the person who abused them. Billy thought Mike was a good friend because he took him places and made him feel special. Billy was hurt and angry about the abuse, but still missed Mike. It's normal and okay to have many different feelings at the same time.

JJ— you better not touch my privates any more. you're not supposed to do that. I don't want you doing that to me any more.

Tim

I hate you. I think your a bum. I really don't like what you did to me. I don't think I can forgive you either.

Mary,

I don't like what you did to me. It makes me feel mad and sad. I will never let you do those sexual things to me again.

Marie

Ideas About How to Protect Yourself

Sometimes it is very hard for kids to know when or how to say "no." There can be many different kinds of situations in which they may find it hard to say "no." Kids have a right to say "no."

For example:

Angela would be very uncomfortable each time her mother would insist that she give her Uncle Joe a kiss because Uncle Joe's kisses made her feel strange and funny. Angela told her mother about her feelings. Her mother said she was glad Angela had told her and assured Angela that she wouldn't make her kiss Uncle Joe or anyone else unless she chose to.

How would you know if someone were talking to you or touching you in a way that made you feel uncomfortable?

_____

_____

_____

What would you do or whom would you tell if.............
A. someone asked you to keep an uncomfortable secret?

_____

_____

B. someone were talking to you or touching you in a way that was not okay and made you feel uncomfortable?

_____

_____

C. something were happening that made you feel uncomfortable?

_____

_____

D. someone ever sexually abused you again?

_____

_____

Write a letter to another kid who has been sexually abused. Give him/her advice.

Date: _____

Dear: _____

I am so sorry to hear about what happened to you. I understand because when it happened to me, I felt _____

_____

My advice is_____

_____

I know what you are going through is really hard because

_____

_____

I wanted to write you this letter to let you know that you are not alone. I hope my advice will help you.

Sincerely,

_____

P.S. _____

_____

Letter From the Abuser

Pretend you are the person who hurt you. What would you like that person to say to you? What would you like to hear?

Date: _____

Dear: _____

I have so many things I need to say to you._____

_____

I have hurt you so much, and I can never make it up to you. It was entirely my fault. In order to say I'm sorry, I would _____

_____

_____

_____

I know that I deserve _____

I know that you may never be able to forgive me and that is okay.

Sincerely,

_____

P.S. _____

_____

Courtroom Drama

Use your imagination and make up a courtroom play or draw a picture about what will happen to the person who sexually abused you.

Date: _____

Judge's Name: _____

Defendant: (the person who sexually abused you)_____

The defendant is sentenced to : _____

for the crime

of: _____

The court is proud of

_____

who was able to come forward
and tell his/her story.

H O O R A Y   H O O R A Y   H O O R A Y

Your Puppet Show

Materials needed:
brown paper bags,
crayons, pencils, scissors,
and a box to use as a stage

You are the director. You are in charge of the show. Make up the characters in your show. Draw and color faces on some brown paper bags and you're ready to go. They can be anyone you want them to be and anything can happen. Act out several scenes. Have one be about what happened to you. You decide what happens when you act it out. You are in charge.

Draw a picture of the person who abused you.

What would you like to do with this picture?

Kids' Poems

I used to think the
   sky was blue
until I saw the likes of you.
You used to hold me very tight
  but then you did those
   nasty things at night
I hate the way you touched me.
I hope you fall from a tree.
             Darlene

I used to trust you
Sometimes you'd let me
Ride in your truck,
I thought I was the one
who had such good luck,
My friends were jealouse
that I had a friend like you.
Why did you do that to me?
I don't understand
Why did you hurt me?
         John

Write your own poem about
what happened to you:

Draw a picture of yourself or write some words describing yourself:

before the abuse

after the abuse

Be an Author

Write a story about a kid who has been sexually abused. What kind of ending do you want your story to have?

Date:_____

Title:_____

_____

_____

_____

_____

_____

_____

_____

_____

_____

_____

_____

_____

_____

_____

How People Feel

Think of some people who know about what happened to you. Draw their faces to show how they feel. You can also write a short story telling about their reactions and feelings.

Getting to Know Yourself

It can be fun getting to know yourself, and it is very important. You can discover things that you really enjoy and like to do. Getting to know yourself can also help you to stay away from situations that you'd really rather not be in. Let's practice getting to know yourself.

1. What are your favorite colors?

_____

_____

_____

_____

_____

2. What are your favorite foods? Your least favorite foods?

_____

_____

_____

_____

3. What is your favorite game?

_____

_____

_____

_____

4. What are some things you like to do?

_____

_____

_____

_____

5. What are some things you don't like to do?

_____

_____

_____

_____

6. What are some things you like about yourself?

_____

_____

_____

_____

7. Who is your best friend? Tell why......

_____

_____

_____

_____

8. Who are your other friends? Tell why.......

_____

_____

_____

_____

9. What are some other things you know about yourself?

_____

_____

_____

_____

Measuring Scale:

This measuring scale is being repeated here so that you and your therapist can be aware of any changes in your thinking, feeling, and behavior. It will help you to know yourself. Circle the word that tells how much of the time you feel or think these things.

<u>Circle One</u>

I feel scared.	Always	Often	Sometimes	Never
I like myself.	Always	Often	Sometimes	Never
I feel sad.	Always	Often	Sometimes	Never
I'm afraid.	Always	Often	Sometimes	Never
I'm embarrassed.	Always	Often	Sometimes	Never
I feel angry.	Always	Often	Sometimes	Never
I'm happy.	Always	Often	Sometimes	Never
I get upset.	Always	Often	Sometimes	Never
I have nightmares.	Always	Often	Sometimes	Never
I'm a good person.	Always	Often	Sometimes	Never
I get mad.	Always	Often	Sometimes	Never
I'm shy.	Always	Often	Sometimes	Never
I have friends.	Always	Often	Sometimes	Never
I like other kids.	Always	Often	Sometimes	Never
People like me.	Always	Often	Sometimes	Never
My family likes me.	Always	Often	Sometimes	Never
I would be a good friend to have.	Always	Often	Sometimes	Never
I'm excited about growing up.	Always	Often	Sometimes	Never

A Journal

A journal is like a diary. It is a place to write down your thoughts and feelings. It helps you to know and understand yourself better! It is a fun way to express your thoughts and feelings. You can use it as a special and private place to keep track of what is going on in your life. You may feel a little awkward at first writing in your journal, but the more you write, the easier it will become. Remember you are a unique and very special person. There is no one else just like you. Writing in a journal will show you how you look at yourself and your life.

Begin on the next page by designing a cover for your journal.

My Journal

Name:_____

Date:_____

My Journal

Record the date each time you write in your journal.

Date: _____

_____

_____

_____

_____

_____

_____

_____

_____

_____

_____

_____

_____

_____

_____

_____

_____

_____

_____

_____

_____

_____

_____

_____

_____

_____

_____

_____

_____

_____

_____

_____

(It would be helpful if you could get a special notebook in which to continue keeping your journal. You can also put pictures in your journal.)

Imagine

Imagine that you go to see a fortune teller. Draw a picture or tell about what your future will look like.

Feelings
Knowing What You Feel

Feelings are very natural and normal. Everybody has them. Feelings are not good or bad; they are not right or wrong. Feelings help us to learn about ourselves. If you pay attention to your feelings, you will know yourself better...what you like and what you don't like...what kind of people and things can make you feel sad, scared, happy, angry, lonely, or joyful. It is very important to listen to the feelings inside of you. It helps to take quiet time to do this.

Here is a list of feeling words:

Sad

Lonely

Confused

Excited

Glad

Afraid

Embarrassed

Surprised

Anxious

Uncomfortable

_____

_____

_____

_____

Other ideas: Add some feeling words to the list. You could also write a story on a separate page and see how many feeling words you can use in your story. On a separate piece of paper, list how many feeling words you can think of that start with the letter

A? B? C? D? E? F? G? H?.........

Feelings

Make up sentences using these feeling words:

You may not know what all of these words mean. If you get stuck, ask your therapist or someone who can explain what they mean.

angry_____

frustrated_____

excited _____

happy _____

sad _____

discouraged _____

thrilled _____

nervous_____

worried _____

jealous_____

ashamed_____

disappointed _____

Anger

It is okay to be angry. It is also okay to express or show your anger. It is not okay, though, to hurt yourself or another person when you express your anger.

Some things that make me angry:

_____

_____

_____

_____

_____

_____

_____

I express or show my anger by:

_____

_____

_____

_____

_____

_____

_____

Being Hurt and Hurting Others

Sometimes kids who are sexually abused are confused and angry. They may try to express these feelings by touching others in sexual ways, hurting others physically, or hurting themselves.

Here is Anna's story:

Anna's babysitter would always make her take off her clothes and play sexual games. Anna was very embarrassed, but never told anyone because she didn't think they would believe her. Anna was very hurt and confused about what happened to her with the babysitter. She wanted someone else to feel bad like she had felt. She began making her little brother and sister play the same sexual touching games. Anna was ashamed of how she was acting. Sometimes she would run away from home, and sometimes she would think about killing herself. Anna finally told her mother about what had happened to her with the babysitter.

What would you tell Anna to do instead of playing the sexual touching games with her brother and sister?

_____

_____

Think of a time you may have wanted to:
A. hurt someone else.

_____

_____

B. hurt yourself.

_____

_____

C. touch someone else in a sexual way.

_____

_____

D. stop living.

_____

_____

If you have any of these ideas or feelings, you need to talk with your therapist or someone you trust right away!

Feelings

What are some things that happen that leave kids feeling:

Happy?

_____

_____

_____

Afraid?

_____

_____

_____

Mad?

_____

_____

_____

Sad?

_____

_____

_____

Excited?

_____

_____

_____

Draw a picture of something that makes you happy:

Draw a picture of something that makes you sad:

**Draw a picture of something
that makes you angry:**

**Draw a picture of something that would be
exciting for you:**

Draw a picture of something that makes you feel afraid:

Draw a picture showing how you could be safe from what you're afraid of:

You are not alone...

You can always ask for help.

Sentence Completion

Finish these sentences.

I like it when _____

I get upset when _____

I feel best when _____

I am _____

I get angry when _____

My dad is _____

My mom is _____

I don't want to _____

I like myself when _____

I cry when _____

The thing I like most about myself is _____

I get sad when _____

I feel ready to _____

I believe I can _____

I know I can _____

My feelings get hurt when _____

Nobody understands that _____

I feel confused when _____

I feel safe when _____

I don't like _____

My family is _____

I have fun when _____

I can _____

My biggest fear is _____

I feel ashamed when _____

When I grow up _____

I'm glad to be me because _____

I am great because _____

Let's Take a Break!

It's important to make time for fun and play activities.

How many words can you find in the word

R H I N O C E R O S ?

example: hose

_____

_____

_____

_____

_____

Word Unscramble

All of these things can be found in an amusement park.

1. REOLRL SEAOCRT   <u>Roller Coaster</u>

2. NTOTCO ANCYD _____

3. OOLP HTE OOLP _____

4. PSOTCUO _____

5. RSIRFE HELWE _____

6. NIRG SOST _____

7. NORPPCO _____

8. LMCRBARES _____

9. TSADR _____

10. UNF EUOHS _____

ANSWERS: 1. Roller Coaster 2. Cotton Candy 3. Loop The Loop 4. Octopus 5. Ferris Wheel 6. Ring Toss 7. Popcorn 8. Scrambler 9. Darts 10. Fun House

CROSSWORD PUZZLE

WORDS IN THE PUZZLE

Lonely

Comfortable

Surprised

Happy

Afraid

Angry

Embarrassed

Confused

Sad

Ashamed

Mad

Anxious

Excited

Glad

ACROSS

1. Feeling lost or like you don't know what direction to take.
3. Feeling scared or frightened.
4. Feeling at ease and like you fit in.
7. Angry.
8. Nervous or tense. Sometimes it means excited.
9. Glad or pleased.
10. Feeling like you can't wait for a surprise.
11. Frightened.
13. Happy.
14. Feeling alone and sad.

DOWN

2. Excited by something you didn't expect.
5. Feeling embarrassed, guilty, or like you've done something wrong.
6. Feeling self-conscious or like you've done something silly.
11. Feeling depressed or down in the dumps.
12. Feeling upset and mad.

Answers on next page

Crossword Puzzle Key

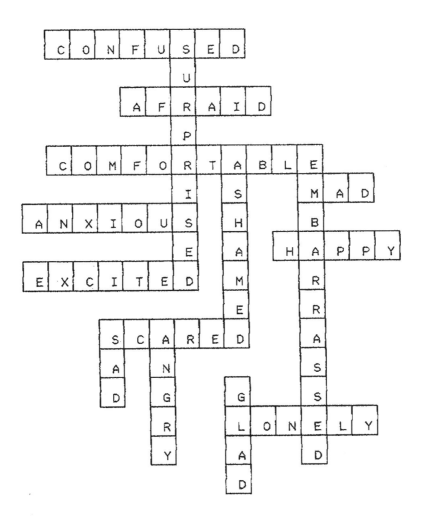

Feelings

Often you will have more than one feeling at the same time. Maybe someone you are close to will do something that upsets you or hurts you. You may feel confused because you love or care about that person, but what they did caused you to be angry or hurt. It's okay and normal to have more than one feeling at a time. Don't try to push feelings down or pretend that you don't have them. Pay attention to your feelings; they are very important.

Example 1.

Katie's mom and dad were getting divorced. Katie had a lot of different feelings at the same time. She loved both of her parents very much. She felt confused, as if she was in the middle and didn't want to have to choose between them. Katie felt very sad about the divorce. She often felt angry because her parents couldn't work things out. Sometimes she worried that it was her fault that they were splitting up.

Can you think of other feelings Katie might have had?

Example 2.

Jimmy liked his Uncle Mike very much. Uncle Mike took him to fun places, bought him things, and let him stay at his house for overnights. Jimmy felt very special to his Uncle Mike. Sometimes Uncle Mike played a game that made Jimmy feel strange. He would touch private parts of Jimmy's body and ask Jimmy to touch private parts of his body. He told Jimmy that the touching game would be a special secret between the two of them. This made Jimmy feel confused. He loved his Uncle Mike, but he didn't like the touching game.

How else do you think Jimmy might have felt?

Can you think of some times when you had more than one feeling at a time? Write them down.

_____

_____

_____

_____

_____

_____

_____

_____

Other Feeling Exercises

1. Name some things that leave you feeling upset and tell why.

   _____

   _____

   _____

   _____

2. Name some things that make you feel happy and tell why.

   _____

   _____

   _____

   _____

3. What kinds of things make you feel angry?

   _____

   _____

   _____

   _____

4. Name some people who help you to feel happy. What do they do that helps you to feel happy?

   _____

   _____

   _____

   _____

5. Tell about a nightmare you had that made you feel scared. Draw a picture of the nightmare. Now think of things that you could do in the dream so you wouldn't feel scared. Draw a picture.

6. What are some things that frighten you? Think of things that you could do to protect yourself or to feel less scared.

_____

_____

_____

_____

Finding Feelings

Find and circle the words in this feeling puzzle. (Words can be found
backwards, forwards, horizontally, vertically, and diagonally.)

```
g  l  a  d  o  s  u  r     p  r  i  s  e  d
   o  n  i  k  m     o  i  l  u  d  n  w
d  n  g  a  l  a     z  v           a  a
   e  r  r  p  r  o     p  o     l  o  l
   l  y  f  p  t  z     i  o     t  o  i
o  y  i  a  n  x  i  o  u  s     y  e  s
u  i  k     n     m  v     u     k  o  a
p        o  c  g     m        l  g  p  d
s  h  y     o  o  r  p  u  h  a  p  p  y
e  c  k  i  p     n  y  o     p  m     i
t  o     j     m     f  s  i  o  z  o  p
y  l  l  i  s  o        u     l  o  d  k
i        p  u  h     l  y  s     l     l
   k     l  k  l  z        e  d  k  l
      l  a  i  c  e  p  s        d     n
p           o  m  m  o     l  z  x  o  p
```

Feeling words to find

The following words may be found in the puzzle.
The key to the puzzle is on the next page.

happy   shy   anxious   sad   silly   angry   confused
upset   afraid   lonely   smart   surprised   special

Key to Finding Feelings

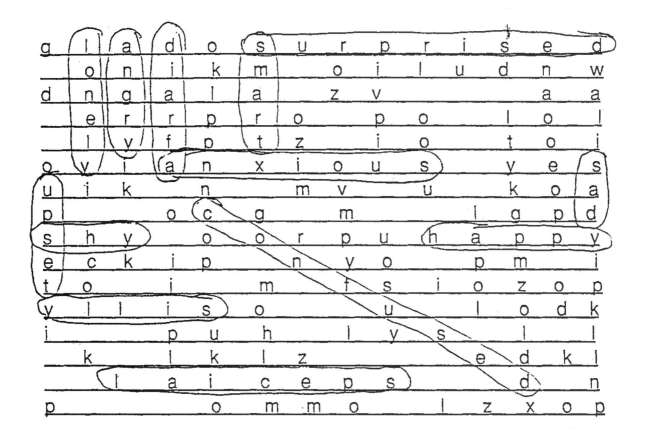

Feelings: Can you match the feeling word with the correct definition? Each answer should be used only once.

1. Happy _____   A.   Feeling like something good is about to happen.

2. Angry _____   B.   Feeling alone and sad.

3. Sad _____   C.   Feeling scared.

4. Afraid _____   D.   Feeling glad about what's going on in your life.

5. Excited _____   E.   Feeling nervous about talking to new people.

6. Lonely _____   F.   Feeling like crying or like there is a lump in your throat.

7. Nervous _____   G.   Worrying about something that might happen.

8. Shy _____   H.   Feeling mad.

Key
1. D
2. H
3. F
4. C
5. A
6. B
7. G
8. E

Meet My Family

These are the people in my family:

(Write down the names and ages of people in your family.)

Tell something about your family.

_____

_____

_____

What are some things about your family that make you feel good?

_____

_____

_____

What are some things that make you sad?

_____

_____

_____

Whom do you usually talk to when you're upset, sad, or afraid? Why?

_____

_____

_____

What would you like to say to your family?

_____

_____

What else would you like to say about your family?

_____

_____

_____

What do you daydream about?

What do you dream about at night?

Self-Esteem: How You Feel About Yourself

20 ways I can enjoy myself:

1. Talk to my family or a friend.
2. Give myself a hug.
3. Get a hug from someone I care about.
4. Take a walk by myself or with a friend.
5. Read a good book.
6. Write in my journal.
7. Do something creative:
   write a story, draw a picture, sing a song, write a poem.
8. Work on a special project.
9. Get some exercise.
10. Watch a movie.

Complete the list with things that you enjoy doing.

11._____

12._____

13._____

14._____

15._____

16._____

17._____

18._____

19._____

20._____

Wishes

1.

2.

3.

Make 3 wishes on this special lantern!

This is Who I Am

Tell about your talents, accomplishments, hobbies, and interests.

Date: _____

Birthdate: _____

Talents: (Things that I can do well)

_____

_____

_____

_____

Accomplishments: (Things I've done well and that I'm proud of)

_____

_____

_____

_____

Hobbies and Interests: (Fun things that I like to do)

_____

_____

_____

_____

Planning Ahead

Sometimes it helps to make plans for things you would like to do. Here is a sample weekly schedule. On the next page you can make up one of your own.

<u>Sample Weekly Schedule</u>

Monday	Tuesday
* Go to school.	* Go to school.
* Do my homework.	* Work in my workbook.
* Go swimming.	

Wednesday	Thursday
* Go to school	* Go to school.
* Call my friends Steve and Bobby.	* Work in my workbook
* Go to baseball practice.	

Friday	Saturday
* Go to school.	* Clean my bedroom.
* Write a letter to my cousin Anne.	* Go to Melissa's
* Walk my dog in the park.	birthday party.

Sunday
* Play and rest.
* Go to church with my family.
* Go out to dinner with my aunt and uncle.

Weekly Schedule of Things I Want To Do

Monday

_____

_____

_____

_____

_____

_____

Tuesday

_____

_____

_____

_____

_____

_____

Wednesday

_____

_____

_____

_____

_____

_____

Thursday

_____

_____

_____

_____

_____

_____

Friday

_____

_____

_____

_____

_____

_____

Saturday

_____

_____

_____

_____

_____

_____

Sunday

_____

_____

_____

_____

RACHEL

Name Plate

Print your name and make a design out of it.

Self-Esteem

Make a list of things you like about yourself.

_____

_____

_____

_____

_____

_____

Make a list of the things you can do well.

_____

_____

_____

_____

_____

_____

How Others See Me and How I See Myself

Draw a picture or write some words telling how you think others may see you.

Draw a picture or write some words telling how you see yourself.

An Art Project For You

Make a collage that expresses your personality: what you like, things you like to do, and things that describe the kind of person you are. In order to make a collage, cut out pictures from magazines.

Color, paint, and/or write words that describe the kind of person you are. Be creative and have fun! If you want more space, use a separate piece of paper.

SUPPLIES NEEDED: paper, scissors, glue, magazines, and crayons, pen or pencil.

Thinking About Yourself

Think about who you are. Pick some words that tell what you're like.
Put a word that describes your personality in each of the circles below.
Next, color in the space around the circle and make a design.

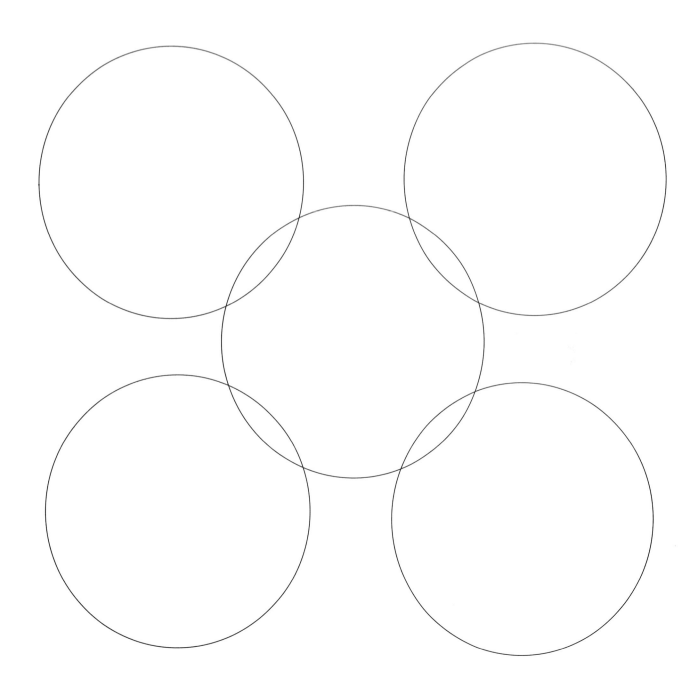

Art Gallery

Draw a picture of yourself or place a photograph of yourself
in the art gallery.

Self-portrait of: _____ (artist)

Be sure to sign your portrait.

Measuring Scale:

This measuring scale is the last one in the book. It is designed to help you see the changes you have made.

Circle One

I feel scared.	Always	Often	Sometimes	Never
I like myself.	Always	Often	Sometimes	Never
I feel sad.	Always	Often	Sometimes	Never
I'm afraid.	Always	Often	Sometimes	Never
I'm embarrassed.	Always	Often	Sometimes	Never
I feel angry.	Always	Often	Sometimes	Never
I'm happy.	Always	Often	Sometimes	Never
I get upset.	Always	Often	Sometimes	Never
I have nightmares.	Always	Often	Sometimes	Never
I'm a good person.	Always	Often	Sometimes	Never
I get mad.	Always	Often	Sometimes	Never
I'm shy.	Always	Often	Sometimes	Never
I have friends.	Always	Often	Sometimes	Never
I like other kids.	Always	Often	Sometimes	Never
People like me.	Always	Often	Sometimes	Never
My family likes me.	Always	Often	Sometimes	Never
I would be a good friend to have.	Always	Often	Sometimes	Never
I'm excited about growing up.	Always	Often	Sometimes	Never

Positive Messages

Say these messages to yourself or out loud.

I am special.

I am loved.

I am a good person.

I don't have to try to be perfect.

I'm great just the way I am.

I am healthy.

I like myself.

I am a good friend.

I am confident.

I can succeed.

People like and care about me.

I am a special and unique person.

I feel good about myself.

I accept myself just the way I am.

I like being me.

Dear Kids,

Congratulations! You have worked very hard on the exercises in this book. We hope that this book has been helpful to you. It is our hope that you realize what a special and unique person you truly are, and we wish you all the best in the future!!!

Sincerely,

Phyllis & Randi

P.S. We will be writing a book with letters and pictures kids have sent to us. If you would like to write to us about your experiences or send us your pictures, we would love to hear from you. Please let us know if you would like your letter or picture to be included in our book. We will not use your material without first getting your permission and your parents' permission. We hope to hear from you!

Please address your letters to: Phyllis and Randi

      C/O Jalice Publishers

      P.O. Box 455

      Notre Dame, IN 46556

Phone list of special friends and people who care about me:

Name   phone number

1. _____   _____

2.. _____   _____

3.. _____   _____

4.. _____   _____

5.. _____   _____

Remember, talking to other people
can really help!!!!!!!!

Certificate of Accomplishment

This is to acknowledge that

_____

has completed work in **Cartwheels.**

Congratulations!

Therapist: _____

_____

Date_____